Greater Than a Tourist
– Austin, TX

50 Travel Tips from a Local

> TOURIST

Noelle Minor

Lock Haven, PA

ISBN: 9781521559130

DEDICATION

To Lucas and Ana,

I love you forever.

BOOK DESCRIPTION

Are you excited about planning your next trip?
Do you want to try something new while traveling?
Would you like some guidance from a local?

If you answered yes to any of these questions, then this book is just for you.

Greater Than A Tourist – Austin, TX by Noelle Minor offers the inside scoop on Austin.
Most travel books tell you how to travel like a tourist. Although there's nothing wrong with that, as a part of the Greater than a Tourist series this book will give you tips and a bunch of ideas from someone who lives at your next travel destination.

In these pages you'll discover local advice that will help you throughout your stay. Greater than a tourist is a series of travel books written by locals. Travel like a local. Get the inside scope. Slow down, stay in one place, take your time, get to know the people and the culture of a place. Try some things off the beaten path with guidance. Patronize local business and vendors when you travel. Be willing to try something new and have the travel experience of a lifetime.

By the time you finish this book, you will be excited to travel to your next destination.

So grab YOUR copy today. You'll be glad you did.

Ten cents of each book purchased is donated to teaching and learning.

CONTENTS

> TOURIST

Author Bio

Noelle Minor was born and raised in Austin, Texas. She grew up running the greenbelt barefoot and playing tag in the isles of the first ever Whole Foods. A true Texas girl; she loves barbeque, horses, and country music.

Most of her days are spent exploring and learning with her two children who she raises on her own. They run up and down the same trails the she did as a child, peruse the shelves of the library, make kitchen experiments, and craft the days away.

She loves reading (when she finds spare time), cooking for the people she loves, and riding horses. She is always up for a camping or backpacking trip, especially if it means she can show off her campfire cooking skills. Roast chicken or paella over the fire, anyone? She is a spontaneous traveler and has a hard time stay settled for too long. She has lived in Spain, Peru, and Mexico. No matter how far she travels, she always finds her way home. Forever the wanderer, she is currently planning her next big adventure.

> TOURIST

WHY AM I A LOCAL?

Austin is home, pure and simple. I am a proud native Austinite. Many people leave their hometowns, but I return to Austin every time because it is special. It holds its own kind of magic. The hot summer sun and cold swimming holes, the smelly bat guano and beautiful people jogging around the lake, the bend-over-backwards friendliness of the locals and twinkling fireflies in the tall grass. Those are what keep me here year after year.

I love that the people here love their animals and live music. I love the long summers and short winters. I love being able to catch a bus to a show or chat it up with a ride share driver and tell him what it was like growing up here. I am curious about the world. I am sure that I will live in other places, but I have no doubt that I will always call Austin home.

> TOURIST

WELCOME TO > TOURIST

> TOURIST

1. *Choose A Great Place To Stay*

When it comes to places to stay, Austin has no shortage of choices. Whether you are in the mood for a luxury hotel or a full-sized short term rental, you are in luck. Downtown, visitors can find The Westin Austin, The W Austin, and The Hilton Downtown Austin. Vacation rentals are scattered throughout the city to fit any budget. Travelers can choose from renovated vintage trailers, sprawling estates, or small post-war remodels. The most iconic Austin spot for overnight guests is the Driskoll. The downtown luxury hotel was opened in 1866 by Civil War veteran and colonel, Jesse Driskoll. Driskoll lost his hotel in a high-stakes poker game not long after and died a poor man. As the story goes, his ghost still haunts the hotel to this day. If you take one of Austin's ghost tours, you'll surely to visit the Driskoll and hear of its founder along with other ghostly Austin tales.

2. *Walk, Run, Or Bike Around Ladybird Lake*

Ladybird Lake was known as Town Lake for decades, and to many locals it still is. Don't get confused when you hear both names referring to the same lake in the middle of town. The trail around the lake is divided into different routes that stretch between two and twelve mile loops. The stunning pedestrian bridge parallel to Lamar Blvd. is strewn with gardens and offers a unique view of downtown. At night, twinkle lights and lampposts light up the trail to a magical effect. Not only can you walk, run, or ride your bike around the lake, but you can also rent a paddleboat, canoe, or kayak for a day on the water. Make sure to wear a swimsuit. Even if you don't accidently fall in, you are likely to want to splash off afterward to escape the Texas heat.

3. Eat Breakfast At A Local Diner

Austin is famous for its local eateries. You can have breakfast any time of the day on any day of the week. There are even a few 24 hour diners that specialize in breakfast fare. Kerbey Lane, a local favorite, has such amazing pancakes that they sell their own mixes (an excellent souvenir!) and they have weekly specials including gluten-free and vegan cakes. Try a side of Kerbey Queso while you are there or, better yet, order the Eggs Francisco. Eggs, bacon, avocado, and tomato on an English muffin covered in Kerbey Queso. Don't forget to add the pancake of the week as one of your sides! Other breakfast spots all have their specialties. Don't be shy – ask the waiter what they recommend. They may be covered in piercings and tattoos, but Austinites are full of Texas charm and Southern hospitality.

4. Grab A Coffee And A Picture At Jo's

Jo's Hot Coffee on S. Congress Ave. is a city landmark. The green wall on the side of the building has the iconic "I love you so much" scrawled on its side. Thousands of visitors stop here every year to have their photo taken. In 2010, local musician Amy Cook wrote the simple sentence in red spray paint on the side of the coffee shop as a love letter to her girlfriend and majority owner of Jo's, Liz Lambert. Due to its already centric location, the graffiti-style mural immediately drew in flocks of visitors. The line to take photos is sometimes longer than the line for coffee, so grab a brew and be ready to wait.

5. Stroll Through The Shops On SOCO

Don't Just leave South Congress Ave., affectionately dubbed SOCO, after grabbing your cup of jo at Jo's. Take a stroll up the hilly street and pop into any number of the unique stores along your way. Here you will find high-end threads at designer clothing shops, antique items and strange found objects at Uncommon Objects, and original Mexican and Latin American Artwork at Tesoro's. Of course, there is plenty to eat in restaurants and trailers along the way. On the first Thursday of every month, local artisans set up tables and booths to showcase their work. Local musicians pound away on drums and walk the streets as troubadours adding a lightness to the atmosphere and filling the air with song.

6. Catch A Flick

Does this sound good to you: sitting back in a thick velvet arm chair to watch a new release with a cold beer in your hand and a burger in front of you? Both Violet Crown, Alamo Drafthouse, and iPic serve up food and drinks to their movie watching patrons. Service is quiet and discreet, so it doesn't interrupt the movie. You'll be surprised at how the servers weave around in the dark with trays of hot food and beverages. Alamo Drafthouse even offers specialty nights with sing-a-longs, classic films, and cult classics. If you have never had the chance to watch Rocky Horror Picture Show on the big screen, never fear. Alamo Drafthouse has your back.

7. Walk Through The Flagship Whole Foods

Whole Foods was born in Austin in a tiny little building on N. Lamar. It moved location, more than once, but now the flagship store sits comfortably on 5th and N. Lamar Blvd. The subterranean parking lot offers ample parking spots for customers. Inside the store, there are various mini restaurants with seating for customers. Brodie Barbeque near the middle of the store has amazing pulled pork and ribs smoked on premises. The rooftop is home to a seasonal ice-skating rink (yes, in Texas!), covered tables, a playground, comfortable couches, and grassy picnic spots. There are numerous free events that take place on the rooftop as well, including free weekly yoga classes. The international Whole Foods offices tower three stories above the rooftop plaza, and if you go around the corner toward the bathroom, you'll find a great view of downtown Austin.

8. Sunbathe Nude At Hippie Hollow

When you think of sunbathing in the nude, you might think of Europe or other exotic locations but I'm willing to bet that Texas isn't the first place to cross your mind. Well, Austin isn't just any old place in Texas. It is special. With that uniqueness comes unique ways to spend the day for both locals and tourists alike. Hippie Hollow, the only clothing-optional park in the state, occupies 109 acres on Lake Travis as a comfortable place for nudists to socialize and soak up the sun. Started in the 1970s as a nudist swimming spot, it has often been mislabeled as a beach, but the rocky limestone embankment is anything but beachy. Most people at the Hollow have a calm and content nature. The atmosphere is laid back and accepting. Maybe it's due to all that vitamin D they're getting.

9. Hike The Greenbelt

The Barton Creek Greenbelt stretches over 12 miles in south-central Austin. Hikers, bikers, and runners easily access the trail heads of Gus Fruh Trail on Barton Hills Dr., Sculpture and Twin Falls on S. Mopac Expressway, Spyglass Trail on Spyglass Dr., and Barton Hills Trail on Homedale Dr. The parking at these access points can be tricky but the natural swimming holes, limestone cliffs, and tree-lined trails are well-worth it. The greenbelt is definitely a local favorite. It is a great place to enjoy the sun, escape the heat, and get a little exercise. People bring their kids, friends, and dogs explore the trails. It is a must-see on any visit to Austin.

10. Visit The Peacocks At Mayfield Park

Mayfield Park is tucked into the north-central neighborhood of

Tarrytown, and throughout its nature trails and small house gardens

peacocks roam. No, they are not native to the area; however, they (and

their ancestors) have lived on the premises for over a century. The

cottage and 21 acres was purchased by former Texas Secretary of State

Allison Mayfield in 1909, though the cottage itself was built in the

1870s. The Mayfields kept the home in the family until the 1970s when

it was donated to the city along with the peacocks that the Mayfields

kept as exotic pets to impress their guests. Today, the peacock

squawking can sometimes frighten visitors to the park if they aren't

expecting it. The few albino specimens there are especially interesting

with their white plumage and red eyes. The females generally sit up in

the trees while the males take the stage, squawking and spreading their

feathers. No matter what, it is a sight for sore eyes. There is nothing

like watching a dozen peacocks strut around like the own the place.

> TOURIST

"People don't live in Austin to work, they work to live there."

Robert Rodriguez, film producer

> TOURIST

11. Make Time For Barbeque

There is nothing like good Texas barbeque, ya'll. Nothing at all.
Plenty of places offer brisket, ribs, pulled pork, sausage, and smoked
chicken but some just simply do it better than others. Texans pride
themselves on their dry rubs and open pit smoking style. At the Salt Lick
in Driftwood, barbeque lovers can watch pit masters smoke up pounds
of meat while they wait for their food. Live country music and twinkle
lights give the place a local flare. Just remember to leave your credit
card behind and bring your own beer cooler, the Salt Lick is cash-only
and BYOB. Another favorite barbeque spot is Franklin's on E. 11th St.
Bring a folding chair and be prepared to wait a while. Doors close when
barbeque sells out which can happen before noon on weekends.
Franklin's has been featured on many food and travel shows. Terry
Black's on Barton Springs Rd. has lunch counter style service and mouth-
watering brisket. Barbeque is so big in Austin that it is hard to drive
anywhere without smelling the smoking meat a few times along the
way.

12. Don't Forget The Tacos

The one thing Austin has more of than barbeque joints is taco stands. The reigning king of Tex-Mex cuisine is the breakfast taco, and in Austin you can grab them in almost any restaurant, café, or food trailer. At the Salt Lick stand in the airport, you can bite into a brisket and egg taco with spicy or mild barbeque sauce. Juan in a Million on E. Cesar Chavez is a little hole-in-the wall joint where you can order a "Don Juan El Taco Grande" which contains the most beloved breakfast taco fillings: bacon, eggs, potatoes and cheese in huge Texas sized portions. There is no shortage of other kinds of non-breakfast tacos either. Rosita's Tacos Al Pastor on E. Riverside Dr. sells traditional Mexican street tacos with al pastor pork cooked on a trompo. El Chilito on Manor Rd. has fluffy puffy tacos filled with savory goodies like carnitas, barbacoa, and boracho beans. Torchy's Tacos began as a small taco truck and now boasts numerous Austin locations. Before going to Torcy's, be sure to look up their secret menu or get ready to try the taco of the month. In March, it's the Roscoe, a taco take on chicken and waffles. Many Austinites wait all year in anticipation for that taco.

13. Swim In The Springs

How do you escape the sweltering heat? Go swimming, of course. There are tons of places to take a dip in Austin, so it is hard to pick a favorite. Some of the best spots are spring fed. The water is cold and refreshing without chlorine or other added chemicals. Barton Springs and Deep Eddy are the most of these popular spots. Barton Springs has a steep hillside that is full of sunbathers all season long, many who go topless or practice acro yoga at the top of the hill. The pool is a rocky and naturally unfinished swimming hole with algae and big diving board. Don't try to go on a Thursday though, the pool is closed in order to protect the native endangered barton springs Salamander which only lives in the pool and a few other close enviorns. The little museum near the pool entrance has some interesting information about the little amphibian. Deep Eddy is another spring fed Austin gem but differs from Barton Springs in that it is set up like a standard pool. The shallow end stretches over half the pool as it gradually increases in depth to 4 feet. Tanned and fit moms are often seen lounging at the edge while their toddlers splash in the cold water with floaties and sun hats.

14. *Watch The Bats Fly*

The Congress St. bridge is hard to miss, and not only because you have a direct view of the capitol building from the overpass, but you can also smell it from far away. Yes, smell. The bat colony that calls the bridge home in the hot summer months goes back to Mexico in the winter and the bats number in the millions. That's a lot of guano. Visitors from all over stand on the bridge every night in the summer to watch the bats fly, but the best places to view them are from below. You can opt for a bat boat cruise on Ladybird Lake which prefaces the bat show with a quick Austin history tour, or you can go the free route and pack a picnic to sit on the hillside below the bridge. The guano smell might ruin any meal you pack though, so it might be a better idea to eat beforehand.

15. *Find Yourself At An International Festival*

Austin is home to not one, but two, huge international festivals. SXSW (South by Southwest) has spots all over the city for wristband holders to listen to music, watch independent films, and take part in interactive technology exhibits. The festival usually coincides with spring break and takes place over a full two weeks. It draws people from all over the world, generally a slightly older and more intellectual crowd than Austin City Limits Music Festival which takes place in the fall. ACL, as it is known, draws megastar bands and is a popular music festival that now covers two separate weekends. Festival goers flock to Zilker park to watch music on multiple stages. It can sometimes be difficult to select who to watch, especially if two of your favorites are playing at the same time.

16. Enjoy A Craft Beer

Like any hipster mecca, beer reigns and craft beer is king. Fancy cocktails and whiskey on the rocks have their place, sure, but there is nothing like a good craft beer. Everyone has their favorite. Whether it is IPA, porter, pilsner, pale ale, or lager there is a delicious craft beer of your liking waiting in Austin for you. Some hotspots for beer lovers are Craft Pride on Rainey St, Barrr on S. Congress, Easy Tiger on E. 6th, and Whip In Convenience Store & Pub on the S. IH 35 frontage road. Did you catch that last one? A convenience store and a pub? Yep, and live music venue and Indian restaurant, too. Maybe Whip In deserves a section of its own here. All of these bars, and plenty others, offer dozens of beers on tap for all of Austin's local and traveling hops lovers. Be sure to try some from the local breweries like Live Oak Brewing, 512 Brewing, and Independence Brewing.

17. Bring Your Pup To Auditorium Shores

To say that Austin is a dog-friendly city would be an understatement. Austinites are borderline obsessed with their dogs. Dogs are allowed in stores and restaurant patios, at swimming holes and city parks. Auditorium Shores is a great example. Located on the south bank of Ladybird Lake near the 1st St. Bridge lies a dog paradise. Every day of the week there are dogs running and catching balls and Frisbees and mingling with other dogs and their owners. It is a great place for dogs to let off some steam and for dog owners to get together and discuss whatever it is dog lovers talk about. Potty training methods and food choices, maybe?

18. Stop At Threadgill's For Gospel Brunch

Threadgill's is a great place to go for some down home southern cooking. They have everything from chicken fried steak and fried okra to cheese grits and biscuits and gravy. Sunday mornings are extra special. The delicious deluxe breakfast buffet comes with a side of live southern gospel music. Deep soul and powerful voices pour over you as you eat a custom-made omelet or sip on black coffee. The musicians often stay afterward to chat with audience members in the dark red booths by the stage. Defiantly make time to wander about the restaurant and lobby while you are there and take in the original records and autographed photos of classic rock icons. Every single one of them preformed at the old Armadillo Music Hall which used to stand just behind the Threadgill's on Riverside Dr. Even though it is no longer there, it's influence is still felt strongly in Austin, the live music capital of the world.

19. Take Your Kids To The Thinkery

There are children's museums and then there is the Thinkery. The big red building in Mueller district houses two stories of hands-on exhibits and activities for kids. The science room upstairs offers experiments at an additional cost while the huge playground offers multi-floors of clear tubes and ropes to climb through. The water room is always a favorite, and they even have vests and water shoes for the kids to wear to protect themselves from getting soaked. You can take a photo of your shadow in the light room or shoot a rocket in the rocket room. It is a great place the take the kids and let them burn off some steam between sightseeing adventures. Across the street, behind the mosaic water creature sculpture, sits another large playground. Beyond even that is Mueller Lake. There are 6.5 miles of trails around the lake, shopping, picnic spots, and even urban fishing.

20. Dig Up Dino Bones At The Nature & Science Center

Tucked away between Ladybird Lake, Barton Springs Dr., and Loop 1 sits a little metal gate in front of some stone steps. If you follow the winding trail past its arch you will find yourself in a little collection of exhibits both housed in small buildings and outdoors. There is quite a surprising range of wildlife exhibits, all of which were are made up of rescued animals native to the area. Some people go for the weekly preschool, and others for the naturalist workshop, but the most well-known attraction is definitely the Dino Pit. This huge limestone pit is sand-filled and houses a few dinosaur skeleton replicas. There are plenty of sand tools and toys for the kids to use as they play paleontologist for the day. It is definitely worth the visit. Head inside to check out the lesser known but equally as cool exhibit at the Nature & Science Center, the specimen counter. This is where people can bring in their found treasures (snake skins, fossils, shells, bones, etc.) and trade them in for points to buy other treasures traded in and on display. Lastly, don't miss the lily pad pond or the creek that winds through the property.

> TOURIST

"I've been surprised by Austin. I had a cowboy image of the place. It's a pretty sophisticated city – in some ways, more sophisticated than Boston. And there's a lighter feel to the place. It's very good for my spirits."

Tim O'Brien, writer

> TOURIST

21. Soak Up The Texas Wildflowers

Every spring, the gently rolling hills of central Texas are blanketed in blues, pinks, reds, oranges, yellows, whites and purples. If go just a little southwest of Austin for a day trip and drive the Willow City Loop, you will be amazed. Bluebonnets sprout at the base of huge prickly pear cactuses beside outcroppings of limestone and kissed by gentle touches of other wildflowers like buttercups, Indian paintbrushes and Mexican blankets. Bluebonnets may be the state flower, but it is the vibrant mixture of colors and petals that give Texas wildflowers their famous beauty. You don't have to leave Austin to see them either. If you happen to be in town in the early-mid spring, you will see them everywhere from the sides of the highway to homes in any neighborhood.

22. Grab Your Partner For A Two Step

Does everyone ride horses in Texas? Well, no, but it still is cowboy country. There may be hipster-clad millennials at every independent coffee house in town but if you step into a place like the Broken Spoke near the very end of S. Lamar Blvd., you'll see the Texas that was here long before kale chips and beard competitions. They serve good food, sure. And a darn good chicken fried steak at that, but the real reason to go to the Broken Spoke is for the two-stepping. The backroom, behind the restaurant, is a slippery wood dance hall with classic country twang and an announcer cheering dancers on. Bring you partner or meet one there, but don't forget to wear your boots!

23. Hit The Bars After Dark

Where do most people think of when they consider going out in Austin? 6th Street, of course. 6th street, the most well-known portion, is some ten blocks that is closed to through traffic after dark. The bars here are one- and two-stories that only sell the most basic beers and cocktails. This part of 6th, also known as Dirty 6th, draws floods of tourists and college students. If you venture east of the highway, you'll find hole-in the wall hipster stops that have pooped up relatively recently over the years. West of Dirty 6th, closer to Congress, you'll find a more professional crowd at nice wine bars and classy restaurants. Many of the customers here work in the tall office buildings that shoot through downtown. Of course, all the action doesn't just happen on 6th. One of its fiercest competitors is the much shorter but just as densely packed Rainey St. There are restaurants and bars of all shapes and sizes on Rainey and even a bar made almost entirely of shipping containers where you can dance the night away. There are many choices when it comes to going out in Austin. Whatever your taste, you'll find a place that is right for you.

24. Visit The UT Tower

Ah, the famous University of Texas Tower. It stands far above campus with its ominous clock that chimes as it warns students that they are late to class, scattering like ants. A visit to campus in general will do you some good. The wide open green of the south mall, the brave squirrels, and the twisting oak trees mix together to give a calming effect even if the campus houses over 50,000 students. If you enter the main building, at the base of the tower, you can ask the visitor center staff about a tour of the tower itself. The tours are $6 a ticket and only run at certain times but the view is not one to be missed. There are taller buildings in Austin, sure, but there is only one UT clock tower. The view of downtown Austin and the UT campus is astounding. The tour itself is self-guided, escorted by UT students, and gives some information on the architecture of the building.

25. Feed The Ducks At Mueller Lake

Mueller Lake is in North Central Austin, across the street from the Thinkery and nestled in the almost Stepford-looking Mueller housing development. Its banks are gently sloped and a great place to take a picnic or read a book under a tree. The 6.5 acre lake is surrounded by concrete walkways and a newly built archway that bridges across the narrowest part of the lake. Large families of ducks glide across the water's surface, and children and adults alike love to feed them day-old bread. Mueller Lake Park also houses all kinds of events for the community like movies in the park, live music concerts, and trout fishing events. There is almost always something going on at Mueller and even when there isn't, it's a great place to go just to feed the ducks and relax on the hillside.

26. Explore McKinney Falls

McKinney Falls State Park is the only state park with campsites located within the city limits of Austin. It is on McKinney Falls Pkwy. between Burleson and William Cannon in east Austin. Just 20 minutes from downtown, you can find yourself walking the comfortable Onion Creek Loop and listening to the sounds of nature. It's a great getaway for a few nights of camping, if you have the luxury of a few days to mellow out by the falls or roast marshmallows by the fire. The upper and lower falls offer two unique perspectives on the seasonal waterway. Another nice aspect of this state park is that the rangers put on plenty of events that are open to the public like night and tree ID hikes, archery lessons, and taxidermy displays. A little side note, McKinney Falls has also been a popular film location in the past few years. The crews of the HBO show "Leftovers" and a movie called "Predator" were two of the most recent to walk the limestone cliffs with cameras and stuntmen.

27. Catch Dinner And A Show At Stubb's

There are plenty of places to go see live music in Austin, and possibly just as many spots to grab some good ol' Texas barbeque, but there is only one Stubb's. Well, technically there are four, but it's the downtown location that draws major headliners to its amphitheater stage. Often, big acts coming to town for larger festivals, like Austin City Limits, will do a show at Stubb's before leaving. The Amphitheater has a great atmosphere for watching live music. The packed earth floor is the perfect dusty dance floor. Other ticket holders watch from wide wood balconies above the restaurant, and strobe lights dance off into the open airspace overhead. The best part? You can grab some ribs or a pulled pork sandwich before the show. What better way to start the night than that?

28. Do Some Graffiti at HOPE Outdoor Gallery

This is arguably one of the coolest spaces in all of Austin. It is a large area of tiered concrete walls where anyone with a spray can is allowed to graffiti anything they want. The ever-changing artwork features stunning and vast murals, quick scribbles, and memorials to people who have passed. Young graffiti artists are given space to practice their skills without fear of retaliation by the police and anyone can go there to admire their work. Many times, people leave behind spray cans and parents let their children pick them up and practice their ABCs graffiti-style. Talk about progressive teaching techniques. What did you expect? This is Austin.

29. See A Play Or Classic Film At The Paramount

The Paramount Theater was built over a century ago in 1915 and housed many acts over the years such as Vaudeville and the 1966 international premier of "Batman." Now, it is mostly used for live plays and musicals by local and traveling performers. In the summer, they host a classic film series that begins with "Casablanca" and ends with "Gone with the Wind", every year. They show James Bond films and Alfred Hitchcock thrillers, even 80s pop icons like Molly Ringwald take the screen some years. Patrons love seeing the old movies with their friends and family and dreaming of what it must have been like when this theater was new and fancy people sat in the opera boxes with their tiny binoculars to watch magicians suspend from the ceiling or take in plays with ladies in tight corsets. Walking into the Paramount is like walking through a portal into another time. It is worth every penny.

30. Visit A Whiskey Bar

Craft beer might be king but whiskey is biting at its heels ready to regain the throne. In recent years, whiskey bars have been popping up all over the country specializing in high class whiskey blends and cocktails. Austin is no different. There are plenty of whiskey enthusiasts amidst the crowds of beer lovers. A few top notch whiskey bars in Austin are the Blackheart on Rainey St. with seductive lighting and stellar old fashioneds, The East Side Show Room on E. 6th with vintage overtones and the entire Pappy Van Winkle whiskey line, and then there is Bar Congress downtown which is small and serious with an almost intimidating air of perfection to their expertly blended whiskeys. No matter which you choose to visit, you have to walk up to the bar with confidence and order the coolest sounding whiskey drink you can think of. If you can think of anything, always go with the old fashioned or just plain old whiskey on the rocks.

> TOURIST

"I like the fact that Austin's the first place I've ever lived where there's a real sense of community. People care about their neighbors."

Ian McLaglan, Instrumentalist

> TOURIST

31. Spin Under The Star At The Capitol

Austin is the capital of Texas, obviously. The capitol building is taller than the one in Washington DC, presumably because everything is bigger in Texas. The dome roof is visible from the top of Congress Ave. but it is invisible from most other vantage points due to the large buildings that now surround it. It is a cool building to visit, literally and figuratively. There are many protests, fundraisers, and rallies held on the front steps, but if you are more interested in what is inside, then you are free to enter. The best part of going inside other than the A/C? Oh that's easy, at least if you are a five-year-old kid. Spin under the star in the main room. When you look up at the five-pointed Texas lone star while spinning, you will topple to the floor. For some reason, this is a Texas capitol tradition. So, I guess that means that if you skip the star spinning, then you kind of missed out on the complete Austin capitol experience.

32. See A Gutenberg Bible At The Harry Ransom Center

The Harry Ransom Humanities Research Center, or the HRC, is located on the University of Texas campus at the corner of Guadalupe and 21st St. Not only do they have original copies of work from some of the most influential writers, artists, activists, and politicians of all times, but they also have a complete copy of the Gutenberg Bible. This is one of only 12 known copies that reside outside of Europe, and one of only 42 in the entire world. It is an impressive sight and is the first item on display after you walk past the front desk to enter the main exhibit. Don't just stop there though, the museum curates excellent rotating exhibits that feature prominent art and artists, activists and history, and inventions and thinkers. The HRC is a great place to decompress and center on the things that truly matter.

33. Wander The Downtown Museums

Aside from the HRC, there are plenty of other notable museums around UT campus and downtown. The Blanton houses floors of fine art and rotating impressionist exhibits. Some of the artists have been featured at the MOMA and Guggenheim in New York. Another great spot is the Texas Memorial Museum on Trinity St. There you will stand under the complete skeleton of a pterosaur, the largest to date of the flying predator from the age of the dinosaurs. You'll probably look up at it and thank goodness that humans were not around at the same time because they definitely would have been easy prey. On the first floor (the basement level), check out the hands-on activities and fossils you can look at under powerful microscopes. There are some other excellent dinosaur bones down below as well. Another favorite, the Bob Bullock Museum which specializes in Texas history on 15th street is a hit with adults and children alike. At the Bob Bullock, be sure to check out the Spirit of Texas IMAX theater and the giant shipwreck on the ground floor. Don't miss the Mexican and Latino art at Mexic-Arte or the stellar community art at The Contemporary Austin, both on Congress Ave.

34. Don't Forget To Bring Cash To Hamilton Pool

Hamilton Pool Preserve is a natural swimming hole just over 20 miles outside of Austin off Highway 71. It is operated by Travis County Parks, so it is outside of the state park system. Be sure to call ahead to make sure the water is good for swimming. On days with high bacteria counts, visitors are prohibited from entering the water. The ¼ mile hike down to the pool is still stunning and worth the mini trek. Also, they are a cash only facility and you might need to reserve your spot ahead of time during high season (summer) through their website. This might all sound like a hassle, but it is surely worth it. The water is cool and refreshing, and has the impressive circular sinkhole of a cenote like those on the Yucatan peninsula. The pool was created when the bedrock collapsed and exposed an underground river due to natural erosion processes thousands of years ago. There is nothing else quite like it in all of Texas, so definitely go have a look and take a plunge.

35. Get Your Craft On

Like scrapbooking? Sewing pillows? Gluing random things together? Using scissors, blocks, and glitter? Well, then CRAFT is the place for you. CRAFT is Austin's crafting workshop. The adults-only space is a place for friends to gather and create. There are both guided workshops and free time in which you can make anything they have materials for, and they have tons of materials. The tall shelves that line and divide the space are filled with all kinds of tools and accessories to put together and make something unique to hang in your house, give as a gift, or place in the middle of your dining table. They even have DIY wedding decoration kits, and they host parties in homes. The possibilities are limitless. Definitely check out CRAFT, and stay to create something special.

36. Live It Up At Lake Travis

Are there any lakes in Texas? Heck yes! Man-made ones, that is. Lake Travis is technically a reservoir of the Colorado River created in 1942 with the construction of the Mansfield Dam in east Austin. The area around it is now a popular spot for large sprawling estates, restaurants, and water activities. You can gab yourself a vacation rental on its banks and enjoy outdoor grilling, sunsets over the water and water sports. Boat and jet ski rentals are a popular attraction at the marinas, and many people come out early in the morning to fish for Bass and Catfish. There are some great spots for camping along the shores of Lake Travis as well. All in all, it is a great place to kick back and relax to enjoy a day or week on the water.

37. Hit A Local Camping Spot

The best camping in the area is done in spring and fall since the summers are so hot, but many people camp year-round here. It never gets too cold to venture outdoors with the proper gear. The most visited campground in the area is probably McKinney Falls (see above) but there are plenty of others which are just as beautiful and pleasant for a nice camping experience. Muleshoe Bend on Lake Travis is operated by LCRA and has fabulous, large sites on the water's edge where campers can bring boats or fishing gear and take advantage of the lovely water. It is also a great spot to snap bluebonnet pictures in the spring. Enchanted Rock, about 1.5 hours from Austin, is an amazing place for a hike or to camp under the stars. The huge granite boulder looks like a small mountain and was once revered as a sacred place by the local native people. Krause Springs to the northwest is also a nice spot. The cool water sits under the shade of large cypress trees and makes for a majestic place. Krause Springs is also great for a day drip and a dip in the cool water. There is no shortage of great camping spots in and around the Austin area.

> TOURIST

38. Head To The Texas Hill Country For A Day Trip

The Texas Hill Country is known for its wildflowers and quaint little towns. The German settled town of Fredericksburg still maintains much of its cultural roots with German names, restaurants, and music. Gruene, Texas is home to one of the best dance halls in the country. You can dance the two step or kick back and tap your toes while you take in the country sounds. Johnson City has the LBJ ranch and farmstead which allow you to step into a fully operational farm and see what it was like in central Texas a hundred or more years ago. There are plenty of other little gems tucked throughout the countryside. Just go for a drive west of town without a plan and see where the road takes you! It's bound to be an adventure.

39. Walk The Trail Of Lights In December

The Trail of Lights is one of the many events that take place in Zilker park every year. It may not be as famous as the annual Austin City Limits Music Festival but it is arguably more beloved by locals and has been running for over 50 years with only a few interruptions. It is a walking trail of Christmas lights that takes pedestrians on a tour of the park; through tunnels, past Santa's workshop, and by dozens of holiday and movie scenes. There is an insane amount of food trailers for your digestive pleasure, but let's be real... you really only need to buy funnel cakes. The trail runs almost the entire month of December form 7pm to midnight. If you go, definitely don't miss the Zilker Christmas tree that stands on a hill across Barton Springs Rd. from the main trail. There is a tree lighting ceremony every year and the whole community is invited. The tradition of spinning around under the tree and staring up at the blurring lights until you fall down dizzy is not to be missed.

40. Get A Hole In One

Is golfing your thing? If so, Austin has you covered. Many people love to golf, and when they travel golf courses are at the top of the list of things they search for online before booking a trip. Never fear, golf fans, we have spots for you! There are some great spots to the west, on Barton Creek. The rolling green hills and waterfront views make this an excellent spot to tee off. Both Fazio Canyon and Fazio Foothills are great spots in the area and back up to the Barton Creek Resort. The golf courses there are challenging, scenic, and edged by wildflowers. There are people who come just to stay at the resort and golf there without even visiting the city once.

> TOURIST

"There's a freedom you begin to feel the closer you get to Austin, Texas."

Willie Nelson, Musician

> TOURIST

41. Try Austin's Favorite Cocktail: The Mexican Martini

Ay, the Mexican Martini. You've never heard of it, you say? Well, then you aren't from Austin, but that's ok. You can try one when you get here. The Mexican martini is a twist on the traditional martini and brings in elements of the margarita to mix it up a bit. Always served in a cocktail shaker with a salt-rimmed martini glass and olive skewer, this drink combines tequila, orange liquor, olive brine, lime juice, orange juice, lemon-lime soda, and sweet and sour mix. Since it is so much larger than a normal drink, customers are often given a two drink limit. A few different restaurants specialize in these classically Austin drinks, but the favorites tend to be Trudy's, Maudie's, Curra's, and Polvo's.

42. Satisfy Your Sweet Tooth

Any true traveler knows that the way to understand the culture is through the food. Well, dessert is its very own food group. There are so many spots for good eats in Austin that it is difficult to narrow down the selection to just a few. If you are looking for ice cold ice cream with interesting toppings, then be sure to hit one of the many Amy's locations where the ice cream scoopers take your toppings and smash them into the ice cream so that they are evenly distributed throughout every bite. Another good spot is a food trailer with a few locations known as Hey Cupcake! What do you think they have there? Cupcakes? Wow, you got it! The cupcakes are sold out of a window in a vintage airstream trailer and they are epic. They are huge, some with ganache fillings, ridiculously moist, and with so many flavors to choose from. Amazing! If you want something a little different from traditional dessert fare, then head to E. Riverside Dr and look for the Churro Co. trailer. This food truck boasts a wide variety of twists on the traditional Spanish churro. Want to try a churro dusted with Oreo sugar, topped with apple pie, or filled with German chocolate filling? I bet you do.

43. Shop At The Domain

There are malls, there are outlet malls, and then there is the Domain. Even the name sounds powerful and daunting, doesn't it? Well it is large and sprawling, yes, but daunting? Not so much. At the Domain you can find boutiques, typical chain mall stores, restaurants, coffee shops, a Whole Foods, and even a long street of bars called Rock Rose. It sounds too good to be true? Well, maybe, but it's not. For those who really love the Domain and the whole north Austin vibe, they even have apartments and condos for rent or sale on the streets that curve through the Domain. Since the whole project was completed just ten years ago in 2007, it's no surprise that everything still looks fresh and new. Four onsite hotels tower above the other buildings and the whole area just feels like luxury. There really is no better place to shop when you go to Austin.

44. Take The Kids To Perter Pan Mini Golf

If you have kids, then chances are they like mini golf and Peter Pan. Well, on Lamar Blvd. and Barton Springs Dr., if you look up past the McDonald's, you will see a giant paper mache looking Peter Pan towering above a mini golf course. With fair prices and fun obstacles, this mini golf is one the whole family can enjoy. The holes haven't changed in decades so it has a vintage quality that some people just love. The faded colors almost look pastel now and the music is always just a little bit crackly over the speaker. Maybe all of that is part of what makes this place so great and so unique.

45. Catch Austin Music Legends

Austin is the live music capital of the world, so it stands to reason that there would be some amazing spots to hear live music. There are plenty of new clubs popping up all the time and restaurants who offer tunes under twinkle lights on their back patios. For a true legendary Austin music spot, look no further than the Continental Club and Saxon Pub. These two bars are both in south-central Austin and are frequented by tattooed bikers, old hippies, and young hipsters. Everyone is welcome, and there is no one type to sit below the stage. Want a unique place to get married? Book the Continental Club. Seriously, you can get married there on stage next to a couple of amps and under flood lights. Some people might even think that's better than Vegas.

46. Expand Your Musical Horizons

After rocking out at the Continental Club you might be in the mood

for some Mozart or Bach. Maybe? Well, if you are, then look at the

schedule for the Bass Concert Hall and the Long Center for the

Preforming Arts. Both venues have concertos, operas, and symphonies

from around the world come and play some of the most delicate and

bold music ever written. You will likely be left breathless as you sit in a

velvet-covered chair in the audience and watch as the musicians move

their bodies, creating something so stunning that it would be difficult to

put into words. The Bass Concert Hall is located on the University of

Texas campus and the Long Center is on Riverside Dr. across from

Auditorium Shores. If you have time, go see a show at both of them

before you leave.

47. Cruise The Local Thrift Shops

Thrift shopping is an art. It is a delicate dance between "oh, no!" and "oh, yes!" It is a weaving past other people in the same aisle and darting in to grab that cute top before they do. Austin thrift shops are no different. There are so many of them here that a person could spend all day thrift shopping and not even touch a quarter of all the thrift stores. There are the traditional spots like Goodwill, Thrift Town, and Thrift Land, but then there are the upscale thrift shops that will only take one or two things out of an entire suitcase of hopefuls to put onto their shelves. Some of these are Buffalo Exchange and Plato's Closet. No matter where you choose to go, you are bound to find something you love if only you sift long enough through the racks.

48. Go Berry Picking

The northern United States might be better for most berries, but in Texas there are dewberries. Dewberries are pretty much just Texas blackberries, but they hold a special place in the hearts of many Austinites. Every year, around May and June, you can head to one of the farms just outside of town and pick dewberries. You load them into little baskets and pay by the pint when you are done. Some of the farms also have peaches and strawberries but their season is even shorter. If you are looking for good peaches, then pick up some at any one of the many roadside stands in the summer. The Fredericksburg peaches are small but they are extremely juicy and as sweet as candy.

49. Do Some Yoga

You might be in Austin on vacation, but staying stretchy and strong is something to work at daily. If yoga is your thing, there are plenty of places you can try while you are in town. If you are lucky enough to come during one of the free series, you can try yoga for free on the roof of Whole Foods. If not, never fear. Black Swan and Practice Yoga have locations around town and run on donations only, so you pay what you can and enjoy top-of-the-line yoga instruction in great spaces and with wonderful teachers. Another place to try is Core Power, especially if you are looking for a major core burn afterward. All the classes are taught in heated studios and target the core. The level I classes can be harder than mid-level classes at other studios. Yoga Yoga has locations all over town as well and they are probably the most traditional of all those listed here. The bamboo floors, soft music, and essential oils give it a truly calming and comforting feeling. You can meditate as you bend. On your way out of class, you will be offered a complimentary tea latte of their making. It is something like a soy chia and a fabulous finish to some awakening yoga.

50. *Watch The Sunset From Mt. Bonnell*

Mt. Bonnell in west Austin is a little hill the looks out over the Lake Austin portion of the Colorado River. The park at the top of the stairs has benches and a gazebo from which to watch the sunset. It is a popular tourist and local spot alike. Some people bring their dogs, others bring friends and family. It is a great place for dates and picnics as well. The best part is definitely the sunset over the water though. The oranges, pinks, golds and purples paint the glassy surface and the sky above and make it difficult to do anything but breath, relax and reflect.

\> TOURIST

> TOURIST
Greater than a Tourist

Please read other Greater than a Tourist Books.

Join the >Tourist Mailing List :
http://eepurl.com/cxspyf

Facebook:
https://www.facebook.com/GreaterThanATourist

Pinterest:
http://pinterest.com/GreaterThanATourist

Instagram:
http://Instagram.com/GreaterThanATourist

Please leave your honest review of this book on Amazon and Goodreads. Thank you.